GW00976014

East Anglian Ragbag
recipes, medicines, home hints, history and poems

MARY NORWAK

Larks Press

This book and its predecessor **'East Anglian Recipes - 300 years of housewife's choice'**

were first published in England by
East Anglian Magazine Ltd. 1978 & 1979.

This new edition is published by
The Larks Press
Ordnance Farmhouse, Guist Bottom, Dereham
Norfolk NR20 5PF
01328 829207

February 1998

Printed by the Lanceni Press, Garrood Drive, Fakenham, Norfolk

Drawings by Lynn Breeze

ISBN 0 948400 68 4

Foreword

Many housewives keep recipe book in which they put cuttings from papers and magazines, or copy out friends' instructions, but these days the notebooks contain nothing else. Until the end of the 19th century, however, it was the custom to keep a 'commonplace' book, and men indulged in the habit as often as women. The book was often thick and well-bound, and in it would be recorded favourite poems, small items of general knowledge, little bits of interesting history, household hints, farm accounts, the meanings of Christian names, lists of good shopkeepers, and of course recipes. Men would record medical prescriptions used in treating their families and their farm animals, but women preferred to record their friends' recipes, beauty hints and simple medicines for coughs and colds.

I have been lucky enought to find a number of these commonplace books, and have pleasure in presenting a second selection from them along with some of my favourite pieces of East Anglian writing to form a Commonplace Book which stretches over 400 years of history in Norfolk, Suffolk and Essex..

MARY NORWAK

Cromer

It is an Ancient Market Town that stands
Upon a lofty Cliffe of mouldruing sands:
The Sea against the Cliffes doth daily beate,
And every tyde into the Lande doth eate,
The Towne is poore, unable by Expence,
Against the raging Sea to make defence:
And every day it eateth further in,
Still wasting, washing downe the sand doth win

That if some course be not tame speedily,
The Town's in danger in the Sea to lye,
A goodly Church stands on these brittle grounds
Not many fairer in Great Britaines bounds:
And if the Sea shall swallow't, as some feare,
Tis not ten thousand pounds the like could reare.

John Taylor (1580-1653)

Wickham Market Easter Sports

On Monday, the 5th of June, a Tea Kettel to
Be Bould For, a Sheme for the Ladies to Run
For, on Tuesday a Badger to Be Baided, After
a Wescote Piece to Be Bould For. A ½ of £b
of Tea to be Bould For By Women, Boys and
Girles. Verious Sports. An ½ a Barrel of Beer
to be Gon a way For the Good of the
Cumpeny. On Wednesday a doncah Race for
a Pannel. Ladies to Run For a Capp. A Band
of Musick to A Blidgen the cumpeny.
Old Newspaper Cutting: about 1825

Rising

Rising was a seaport toun
When Lynn it was a marsh.
Now Lynn it is a seaport toun
And Rising fares the worse.
Old Rhyme

To Pot Cow Heels

Take cowheels and boyl them wery tender then
take the meat from the bones and strow some
pepper and salt enough to season them. Put
them hard down into a pot let them stand till
cold then set the pot to the fire and keep it with
turning till you can shak it out then put it into
souce drink made of small bere and salt.
Elizabeth Ravell: 17th century
Suffolk/Essex border

****Souse drink was sometimes a salt brine, or
else a mixture of wine or beer with salt in
which meat was immersed. The salted wine or
beer was taken as part of the dish and was
particularly popular for the Christmas feasting
of Elizabethan farmers. There is a survival of
this dish in the serving of brawn with salt,
pepper and vinegar.**

Blakeney

As in her days of power and state,
The great church stands, uplifting high
Her lantern - long the guiding eye
Of commerce - Surely they were great
Who could so build, and, day by day,
From sheltered homes could valiantly
Go forth to meet so wild a sea
As that which booms beyond the bay.
Those days are gone. There sound no more
The capstan song, the welcoming hails,
As some stout trader, fraught with bales
From Eastland marts, draws near the shore.
For not to Anglian ports today
Turns England with her swollen needs.
They perished, but they sowed the seeds
Of empire ere they passed away.
Not all has gone; the marsh and lea
Still the migrating myriads flock,
To preen their plumes, and ease the shock
Of their long battling o'er the sea.
Not all is lost for Beauty flies
From hearts that keep no place for her,
And with the wild sea-lavender
Builds here a home for outraged eyes,
That late have looked where, seamed and scarred,
Lies what men reverenced once. May all
Who hear the bells of Blakeney call,
Against a like despoiling guard.
Thomas Thornely (1855-   )

To Make Shrub

Take 6 lemons peiled and slised very thine put them into a quart of brandy and the rine of on of them. Steep them 24 hours then add 3 quarts of sider let them stand 12 hours together then drain them through a fine sieve then put 2 pounds of fine suger lofe suger let the whol stand a while together then take it as clear from the bottom as you can then bottle it. After that drink it according to discretion.

Elizabeth Ravell: 17th century
Suffolk/Essex border

Norfolk Ghosts

There is a family ghost at Wolterton, which at intervals is seen by old servants about the place. A white lady is said to be in the habit of appearing whenever some calamity is about to threaten our family. Some little time before my brother, the late Lord Orford, died, in 1894, I well recollect his saying to me: 'I hear from Norfolk that the white lady has been seen again. It is you or I this time, Dolly, for we are the only ones left.'

The white lady in question is supposed to be one of the Scanler family, who were the possessors of Wolterton before my ancestor built the present mansion. There used to be some story that one of the Lords Orford unearthed the old tombstones of the Scanlers in the ruined church in Wolterton Park, and that this act of sacrilege was the cause of the poor lady's spirit being so disturbed. But I have recently discovered that no act of this kind was ever perpetrated at all, so it must have been for some other reason that the ghostly dame lingers about Wolterton Hall. In the old days the Walpoles used to be driven in their hearse three times around this ruined church before being laid to rest in the family vault. A ghost of much more tragic mien is supposed to haunt Mannington, another house close by, at which my brother used to live, for there it was that Dr Jessop declared that he had seen the ghost of Henry Walpole, the Jesuit.

Reminiscences of Lady Dorothy Nevil (1906)

To Make Anything Waterproof

Dissolve 1 lb alum, 1 lb sugar of lead in a bucket of cold water, ½ the quantity for 2 gallons of water. Stir until quite dissolved, allow any sediment to settle and pour off the liquor. With a brush apply the liquor liberally to the textile and hang out to dry, not wringing out the moisture but allowing it to drip. If ironing is necessary do it on the wrong side.

Household Recipe book, Norfolk (early 20th century)

Old Yarmouth

September 6th, 1596: None shall bring boys or wenches from the north into the town on pain of imprisonment. The town being greatly annoyed with hogs, geese and pigs, ordered that the crier shall give warning to keep them up, or after eight days any man may kill such hogs, geese, &c., and to have 12d for a hog, 6d for a goose for his trouble.

March 24, 1608: Ordered, that no inhabitant shall go over the bridge to buy any goods, wares and merchandizes, and if any shopkeeper offend therein after being warned, shall forfeit the goods bought.

May 6th, 1632: The order made that all aldermen's wives wear velvet hats henceforth revoked.

Orders made in the reigns of Elizabeth I, James I and Charles I and recorded in the Old Assembly Books of Yarmouth.

Eau de Cologne

1 oz essence bergamot; 1 oz lemon peel; 1 oz lavender; 1 oz orange flower water; ½ oz essence cinnamon; 15 oz spirit of romary; 15 oz spirit of melissa; 7½ pints alcohol. Leave to stand for 14 days. Distill in retort.

19th century Household Book, Essex

The Language of Food

APPLE-JOHN OR FLAP-JACK. Sugared apples, baked in a square thin paste, the two opposite corners flapped, or turned over.

BANG. Suffolk Cheese, made of milk several times skimmed. *Trip, Wommill* and *Thump* are other local names for it. Its toughness has given rise to a number of local illustrations. In one, the cheese exclaims:

> *Those that made me were uncivil,*
> *For they made me harder than the devil;*
> *Knives won't cut me; fire won't sweat me;*
> *Dogs bark at me, but can't eat me.*

'Hunger will break through stone walls, or anything except Suffolk cheese' is a proverb from Ray. Mowbray says 'it is only fit to be cut up into gate latches, a use to which it is often applied.' Other writers represent it as most suitable for making wheels for wheelbarrows.

BEVER. The afternoon snack of harvest men and outdoor workers. A Suffolk workman's *extra* meals, as looked for at gentlemen's houses, consist of *leveners, noonins* or *nunshens, bevers* and *foorzes,* exclusive of sundry little interjectional stimuli and interpolations under the head of *whets, baits, snaps, snacks,* and *snatches,* relieved by *Lowans* or beer.

BONX. To beat batter for puddings.

BOTTLE-BIRD. An apple rolled up and baked in a crust.

CHATE, CHOAT. A feast, treat, rustic merry-making, jolly frolic.

COOK-EEL. A sort of cross bun made and eaten in Norfolk during Lent.

COST or COAST. Ribs of cooked meat.

CRAB-LANTHORN. A pasty of the apple-jack type.

DOWLER. A sort of coarse dumpling.

ESSEX MILES. These are cried up for very long, understand it comparatively to those in the neighbouring country of Middlesex *(Fuller's Worthies).*

> *Essex Miles, Suffolk Stiles, Norfolk Wiles*
> *Many Men beguiles.*
> *Old East Anglian Saying*

GIRTY-MILK. Porridge of oatmeal or grits.

HARVEST-BEEF. Any kind of butcher's meat, eaten in harvest.

HOLLOWMEAT. Poultry, rabbits, game not sold by butchers.

HOT POT. Warmed ale and spirits.

JUMP-SHORT. Mutton from sheep drowned in the fen drains.

JUNKETS. Dainties, delicacies.

KICHEL. A flat Christmas cake, triangular, with sugar and currants strewed over, given to children by their godfathers.

MARTLEMAS-BEEF. Beef salted and dried up the chimney.

NOG. A sort of strong heady ale, peculiar to Norwich.

PUDDING-PYE-DOLL. The dish called toad in the hole, meat boiled or baked in a crust.

ROB. Jam, thick jelly made from fruit.

RUDLE. A beverage composed of warm beer and gin, with sugar and a slice of lemon peel.

SKRUSSLE. The hard crackling skin of a roast loin of pork, breast of veal, &c.

SOUPINGS. Any sort of spoonmeat.

STULL. A luncheon, a lump of bread or other eatable.

SWARD-PORK. Bacon cured in large flitches.

TANTABLET. A fruit tart with its surface tricked out with shreads of pastry.

WATER-WHELPS. Dumplings boiled sad, or kneaded without yeast or eggs.

YARMOUTH CAPON. A red herring.

John Greaves Nall, Chapters on the East Anglian Coast (1866)

Early W.I. Hints

MOP FOR FLOOR.
6d mophead, dip it into paraffin and leave it out of doors till all smell has gone.

TO MAKE COAL GO FURTHER.
Mix ½ lb soda in pail of water, throw over coal before using.

TO MAKE WASHING SOAP.
Mix mutton fat and 95% soda, put them together lukewarm.

FOR SCENTED SOAP.
Collect odds and ends of scented soap, cut them up and melt in a jar stood in boiling water. If soap is very dry, add a little water, to this mix heaped teaspoon fine oatmeal and teaspoon olive oil.

TO KEEP AWAY RATS. Mix cement and waterglass, plaster over rat hole, it hardens like iron. Put aniseed in hole first.

MAKE OLD UMBRELLAS into clothes airers.

TO MAKE LOAM. 1 part sand, 1 part animal matter, 2 parts leaf mould.

TO CURE SKINS. Get skins from Nov. to March. Teaspoon alum and teacup salt, rub with mixture for 2 days, wash it in soft soap and lukewarm water and hang out to dry, not too sharp a dry. Rub with teaspoon alum and teaspoon alum and teaspoon borax. Another way for sheep skin, car. soda 1 part, Hudson soap 2 parts, powdered alum 3 parts, dust over for a week. Or skins can be put into the following mixture for 4 or 5 days to wash 1 lb salt, 1 oz alum, teaspoon saltpetre to 2 quarts water, powder with alum and borax. To soften a hard skin, ½ pint boiling water, ½ teaspoon salt, ½ tablespoon burnt alum, ½ teaspoon unslaked lime. Stir till dissolved and brush over the skin, it may be done 3 times but must be done hot.

Household Recipe Book, Norfolk (1920-40)

**The household recipe book quoted begins in the early 20th century with Victorian family recipes and progresses through the more economical and indeed difficult times of the 20s and 30s. The final 'hints' culled from W.I. meetings between the two World Wars indicate that old ways died hard, with the housewife remaining a versatile creature who* made her own floor polish, mended pans, dispersed rats, made soap and cured sheepskins.*

Dr Tillotsons Wives Water For Convulsiv Fits

To one quart of ye very best white wine put four ounces of single paony root scraped and sliced then lett ym infuse in ye wine 24 hours yn strain ym oute put into the liquor 24 grains of a dead mans skull finely powdered and 16 grains of ye moss yt grows on a dead mans skull one ounce of ye spirit of caster half an ounce of ye powder of castor. When you have put all these in shake ym together one hour and as often as you take it. Dosing 2 spoonfuls for a man 2 for a woman and a small one for a child, in ye morning fasting three days before and three days after ye new and full moon and just before ye fit comes.

liEzabeth Ravell: 17th century
Suffolk/Essex border

***The lichen and moss from a dead man's skull was sometimes called 'mummy' and was included in medical prescriptions until the 18th century. The skulls came from embalmed corpses, and the moss was considered a sure cure for bleeding, and the prevention of putrefaction.*

Hay

I think that we shall never know anything more fragrant than hay. From its earliest growth in the meadows to the season of haysel it is beautiful. The building of the rick, its thatching, its cutting up into trusses, the proper loading of the wagon - all these were good subjects for the pencil of the artist and were among the many highly-skilled trades co-ordinated with the primal trade of farming.

Very pleasant, too, in my memory was its passing at night through Suffolk and Essex to the hay-markets in London whose streets thenadays were thronged with horses. I have been soothed on many a wakeful night to peaceful slumber by the gentle sound of the wagons passing through the village street beneath my window; hearing the familiar woody chuckle of the heavily laden axles, the rattle of the swinging bucket beneath and the steady clip-clop of the horses' hooves steal out of silence to a full crescendo as they passed; then slowly the sounds diminished far away along the country road again. It was mostly a night journey and the train of wagons and carts often stood in the evening outside the King's Head long enough for me to fix them in the sketch-book.

George H. Rose
Pages from the Sketchbook of an East Anglian Artist (1948)

To Make a Quaking Puding

Take a pint and somewhat more of thick creame tenn eggs, 3 whites, beat them well with 2 spoonfulls of rose water. Mingel with your creame 3 spoonfuls of fine flower let there be no lumps in it. Put it all together and season it to your tast. Butter a clorth very well and let your clorth be thick that it may not run out. Let it boyl half an hour as fast as you can then take it up and make sauce for it with butter and rose water and suger and serve it up you may stik it with blanched almons if you please.

Elizabeth Ravell: 17th century
Suffolk/Essex border

Roll Up! Roll Up!

To the Nobility, Gentry and Etc.
Who are admirers of the extraordinary
Productions of Nature to be Seen
During Bury Fair, at the
Bottom of the Angel Hill

Maria Theresa

The Amazing Corsican Fairy
Who has had the honour of being shown three times before Their Majesties. She is only 34 inches high, weighs but 26 lbs. and is allowed to be the finest display of Human Nature in miniature that was ever shown in England. To be seen from ten in the morning till nine at night. Gentlemen and Ladies, one shilling; servants, etc., sixpence. During the present time of St. Edmund's Bury Fair, will be exhibited in a commodious Booth, on the Angel Hill, facing Cook Row, the capital collection of living wild Productions which were shown all last winter, facing Temple Bar, London, with several additions. The famous Lion combatant, who in a few weeks is to encounter many Bull Dogs, being matched by two noble personages for a large sum of money: a young He Lion not above ten weeks old, so that the curious may now have an opportunity of that which will not present itself again in an Age of taking a Lion in their arms, etc. The celebrated Oriental Tyger, which is as large as many heifers, and as beautiful as the Queen's Zebra. There is likewise a multiplicity of other extraordinary Phenomena.

Suffolk Playbill

To Dry Cheyres (Cherries)

Take two pound of cherys. Stoon them and put them into a silver dish then take 6 spoonfulls of the juce of cheryes. Put to them a quarter of a pound of suger finely beaten. Strew in on them let them boyl till they be cleare, when take them out and lay them one by one in a dry dish. Keep them safe in an oven still turning them till they be dry.

Elizabeth Ravell: 17th century
Suffolk/Essex border

Praise of Woeman Kinde

Can man be silent and not praise finde
For her that lived the praise of woeman
           kinde
Whose outward frame was lent the world to
           gess
What shapes our soules shall weare in
           happiness
Whose virtue did all ill so overswaye
That her whole life was a Comunion Daye.
John Donne
Lines on a memorial to Dame Katherine Paston, Paston Church, Norfolk (1629)

Ballooning

On Friday, the 23rd of July, 1785, at half past four, Major Money ascended in a Balloon, from the public garden without St Stephen's gates, Norwich and passing over Pakefield, a village between Yarmouth and Southwold, was carried near seven leagues from the land before the balloon touched the water...and after beating about for four hours, was extricated from his perilous situation by the Argus revenue cutter.
Norfolk Tour 1795

To Preserve Cucumbers

Take small cucumbers and large ones that will cut into quarters let them be green and as free from seeds as possible, put them into strong salt and water, that will bear an egg, in a narrow mouthed jar with a cabbage leaf to keep them down and tye a paper over them and set them in a warm place till they are yellow, then wash them and set them over the fire in fresh water and a little salt with a cabbage leaf over the top, cover the jar close and take care they do not boil, if they are not of a fine green change your water which will help them, then make them hot and cover them as before, when they are of a good green, take them off the fire, let them stand till they are cold, and then cut the large ones into quarters taking out the seeds and soft parts, and then put them in cold water, and let them stand 10 days, change the water twice a day to take out the salt - take a pound of double refined sugar and half a pint of water, set it over the fire when you have skimmed it clean put in one ounce of Ginger, when your syrup is getting thick, take it off the fire, when cold wipe the cucumbers dry and put them in, boil the syrup once in two or three days, and strengthen if it required, as the greatest danger of spoiling them is at first.

Elizabeth Hicks: late 18th century Suffolk/Essex border

Cock-fighting in Norfolk

The annual great main of cocks between the gentlemen of Norwich and Northamptonshire for £5 a battle and £200 the odd, will be fought at the White Swan Inn, St Peter Mancroft, Norwich, on Tuesday, April 22nd, and two following days. A silver tankard will be fought for by 16 subscribers. No cock to exceed four pounds ten ounces. The above to be fought in fair silver spurs, and to commence fighting each day at twelve o'clock. Feeders: Nash for Northampton, Skipper for Norwich.

Advertisement in 'Norfolk Chronicle' (1823)

**The earliest record of cock-fighting comes from FitzStephens of London who died in 1191. He described Shrovetide cock-fights staged in all the London schools by the boys who brought fighting cocks to their masters, and matches were fought in front of many spectators. It was known as the 'Sport of the Sod' and was a royal pastime with a cockpit in Whitehall. In East Anglia, the sport was enjoyed by Charles II at Newmarket, and the Coke family were Norfolk devotees. At the beginning of the 19th century, Holkham tenants had to give two fighting-cocks as part of their rents. Matches were staged throughout Suffolk and Norfolk in such inns as the Black Boy at Aylsham, the White Hart at Swaffham, the Red Lion at Fakenham and the Sun at Wells, and results depended on the feeder. Mr Nash fed the birds on stale bread soaked in boiling ale and fortified with port, sherry and other wines.

Ipswich Apricot Mincemeat

1 lb of dried apricots, 1 lb cleaned currants, 1 lb boxed dates, 1 lb raisins, 1 lb cooking apples, 1 lb demerara sugar, 2 oz Jordan almonds, ½ teaspoon grated nutmeg, ½ teaspoon ground cinnamon, ½ teaspoon ground cloves, 1 large lemon, 2 tablespoons brandy or whisky.

Wash apricots thoroughly, then drain. Soak in cold water to cover for 12 hours. Drain thoroughly, then chop finely. Add currants. Stone dates and raisins and chop roughly. Add to apricot mixture. Peel, core and chop apples. Place in a basin. Add the sugar, almonds and spices. Grate in the rind of lemon, then extract and strain the juice. Add apricot mixture. Stir thoroughly till blended. Cover. Stand for 2-3 hours, then stir in the brandy or whisky. Pot and seal. Store in a dark, dry and airy pantry. An old family recipe.

Miss Longhurst, Cley-next-the-Sea, Norfolk (1979)

Newmarket

How my hearte beats with eager speed!
What joy in man! How neighs the steed!
Unstabled hunters scour the plain.
Young Piper there would stretch the rein.
Lay by the law, resign the gown,
For rural sports exchange the town.
The spring serene does friends invite,
To mix with thousands in delight.
She that in the chariot rides,
He who the fretful horse bestrides:
The heir, that on the turf rebounds,
Which to the hoof or wheel resounds;
Crowds that from Newmarket spread,
And o'er the heath confus'dly tread.
Why all these sporters in your eye
List to the word impetuously
'They're off, they're off', now here now gone,
And quick the vig'rous race is run.
Scarce breath allow'd, or time to lay
Who loses or who wins the day.

Kenrick Prescot (1770)

To Make Sugerrolls

Take a pound of flower a pound of suger six
eggs and keck them with beating till your
oven be hot when put your butter into your
pan and so bake them.

Elizabeth Ravell: 17th century
Suffolk/Essex border

Wartime Christmas Cake

November 17th: Store cupboard now resembles
Mother Hubbard's as far as fruit is concerned
but the Christmas cake is just out of the oven.
The recipe has been used in the family for
years, examples travelling overseas to Egypt in
World War I, and would keep for 12 months in
a tin at home. It needs 12 oz. flour, 8 oz.
butter, 8 oz. sugar, 4 oz. each currants, peel,
sultanas, 2 oz. glacé cherries, grated rind and
juice 1 lemon, 3 eggs, teaspoon baking powder;
baked in medium oven two or three hours.
Have used margarine instead of butter in mine.
But this will not be expected to keep long!

*Elizabeth Harland's diary: Eastern Daily Press,
1940*

Lynn Breeze

Pills

1 pound of loafe sugar finely beaten and
searsed (sieved), 3 ounces of penioes, 1
ounce of orris root, half an ounce of cole
fine powdered and searced, half an ounce of
brimstone. Drop upon all those powders five
drops of oyl of anniseeds then dissolve one
ounce and half of liqquorish balls in four
spoonfulls of hyssop water and so put to ye
powders and mix with them as well as you
can. Then add so much of gum tragacanth
steepd in rose water as will make it into a
stiff past, put not to much gum in att first, a
pennyworth will be to much steeped in 7 or
8 spoonfulls of rosewater, make ye past into
small rolls and dry ym in ye sun or stove.

Elizabeth Ravell: 17th century
Suffolk/Essex border

To Make Surrup of Horehound good for Colds or Horsness

Take 2 good handfulls of the hearb horhound
2 handfulls of blew figgs 2 handfulls of
raysons stoned 1 ounce of liquorish brused.
Boyle all this in 2 quarts of spring water will
half be consumed then strain it and put to
the liquor on pound of good suger and boyle
it to a full surrup. You may take it at any
time of night or morning or both if need
require.

Elizabeth Ravell: 17th century
Suffolk/Essex border

An Apoplectick Dart

Here lies the body of Bridgett Applewhaite
once Bridgett Nelson
After the Fatigues of a Married Life
Born by her with Incredible Patience
For four Years and three Quarters bating three
Weeks
And after the Enjoyment of the Glorious
Freedom
Of an Easy and Unblemish't Widowhood
For four Years and Upwards
She Resolved to run the Risk of a Second
Marriage Bed
But Death forbad the Banns
And having with an Apoplectick Dart
(The same Instrument with which he had
Formerly Dispatch't her Mother)
Touch'd the most Vital part of her Brain
She must have fallen Directly to the Ground
(as one Thunderstrook)
If she had not been Catch't and Supported
By her Intended Husband
Of which Invisible Bruise
After a Struggle for above Sixty Hours
With that Grand Enemy of Life
(But the certain and Merciful Friend to
Helpless Old Age)
In Terrible Convulsions, Plaintive Groans or
Stupefying Sleep
Without Recovery of her Speech or Senses,
She dyed on ye 12th day of Sep.
In ye year of our Lord 1737 of her own
age 44.
Memorial in Bramfield Church, Suffolk

Buckworths Lozenges

Take the powder of anneseeds of liqquorrish of
orrice of each a quarter of an ounce, angelica
elicumpain (elecampane) powdered of each half
a quarter of an ounce, half a quarter of an
ounce of flower of sulfer 6 drops of oil of
amber, 6 drops of oil of sasefries (saxefrage).
Make them into lozenges with on pound of
good suger. Melt your suger in a quart skillet
with 6 spoonfulls of water make it boyle a little
then put in all the powder and oyrls and boil
them apace till it be suger again, then power it
on a piplate that have bin rubed with a little
butter to keep them from sticking. When they
are almost cold cut them into what form you
please.
*Elizabeth Ravell: 17th century
Suffolk Essex border*

To Make Black Puddings

Boiled in milk quarton of oatmeal, lemon
thyme, sweet marjoram, pennyroyal, leeks,
fennel, nutmeg, cloves, mace, Jamaica pepper
(allspice), 10 eggs (only half the whites),
orange flower water 2 pennyworth, small glass
of brandy, 2 pennyworth of bread greated, little
blod, a great deal of fat, a littel salt.
Martha Smith's book, Essex (1756)

Lettuce

Oh! Cruel death to please thy palate,
Cut down Lettice to make a sallet.
*Tombstone memorial to Lettice Manning
(1737) in Moulton, Suffolk, churchyard*

Suffolk Churches

I like churches for the shape of them, the
setting of them, their splendour or their
quaintness. Odd and lovely things attract me
in churches: the Great Dome at Wenhaston;
the font covers at Worlingworth and Ufford;
the tombs at Dennington, Framlingham and
Wingfield; the bench-ends at Fressingfield
and Woolpit; the humorous inscriptions at
Bramfield and Boxford; at Boxford again the
brass of a child asleep in a four-poster bed,
and at Lavenham the tiny one of a baby
wrapped in swaddling clothes. These and a
hundred other strange objects I have seen in
various corners of the county. I must have
visited three-quarters of the churches in
Suffolk; but I search their interiors for the
effects of shape and light and delicacy, and
not to hold post mortems on their anatomies.
Julian Tennyson, Suffolk Scene

Dunwich

Last of a score of towers,
To fling defiant music o'er the sea,
That Lion-like roared round and now devours,
Thy vigil ends, Dunwich has ceased to be!

E'en while she crowned her state
With mitred pomp in her meridian day,
The foe had rolled his thunders to her gate
And hurled afar the challenge of his spray.

And now we mourn the fall
From lone sea-bluff of her last lingering
shrine;
It fell, as on Bysantium's ruined wall
Fell, midst the Paynim, Rome's last
Constantine.

Beyond that ruthless main,
Still, swollen or shrunk, her old-time rivals
stand,
But they that Dunwich seek shall seek in vain,
They find but moaning sea and shifting sand.
Thomas Thornely (1855-   )

To Macke a Cake

Tack a quarten of flour, rub in to it a lb of
butter, ½ lb lard, 2 lb currants, 1 lb sugar, 3
eggs, 2 pints milk, wine and brandy a tumbler
of each. Nutmeg, cinamon, cloves and mace,
salt and barm (yeast).
Martha Smith's book, Essex (1756)

Turkey Walking

Suffolk is particularly famous for furnishing the
City of London and all the counties round with
turkeys, and it is thought there are more turkeys
bred in this county, and the part of Norfolk that
adjoins it, than in all the rest of England. A
person living in this place has counted 300
droves of turkeys (for they drive them all in
droves on foot) pass in one season over
Stratford Bridge on the river Stour which parts
Suffolk from Essex, about six miles from
Colchester on the road from Ipswich to London.
These droves generally contain from three
hundred to a thousand each drove, so that one
may suppose them to contain 500 one with
another, which is 150,000 in all; and yet this is
one of the least passages, the numbers which
travel by Newmarket Heath, and the open
country and the forest, and also the numbers
that come by Sudbury and Clare, being many
more.

They have found it practicable to make the
geese travel on foot too, and it is very frequent
now to meet droves with a thousand, sometimes
two thousand, in a drove. They begin to drive
them generally in August, by which time the
harvest is almost over and the geese may feed
in the stubbles as they go. Thus they hold on to
the end of October when the roads begin to be
too stiff and deep for their broad feet and short
legs to march in.
*Daniel Defoe, Tour Through Great Britain
(1724)*

To Make a Seed Cacke

To 10 pound of flower you must put ten
eggs a quart of cream a quart of butter.
Warme your cream and melt your butter, 2
pound of suger, a pound of carriway comfits
a quart of ale yeast, oring peale, six turn
ringaroot (eringo root). When your oven is
almost hot, mix well together, make it a stiff
as you do a pudding so put it into your
hoope, let your oven be well hot.
*Elizabeth Ravell: 17th century
Suffolk/Essex border*

To Keep Green Peas till Christmas

Shell your Peas and put them into boiling
water with some salt, let them boil for 5 or
6 minutes then put them into a Cullender to
drain, double a cloth thick on a table and
spread them on to dry, then fill your bottles
cover them with Mutton fat when it is a little
cool fill the necks almost to the top, cork
them tie a bladder over them and set them in
a cool dry place. When you boil them put
them into the water hot with a little salt,
sugar and a piece of butter.
*Elizabeth Hicks: late 18th century
Suffolk/Essex border*

How to Stew Chickings

Take a peck of oysters and the liquor and on pint of whit wine a little hole pepper some large mace 3 anchovies an onyon. Let your chickings be almost boyled first in water with a little otmeale to make them look white, then take them out and make your oysters boyl then put in your chickings and let them stew together will your oysters be tender then put in a good peace of sweet butter. Let it not boyle after the butter is in, thick it with the yealk of 6 eggs well beaten with a spoonful of the lyquor they are stewed in.

Elizabeth Ravell: 17th century
Suffolk/Essex border

To make a Cold Hash

Take the flesh of a cold turkey or of a loyle (loin) of veale cut it in peaves as bige as oysters but very thin. Put to it sum capers cut small and anchovies a little pepper sum lemon cut small 3 or more spoonfulls of vinegar 2 spoon of good oyle salt accordind to your tast. Shake them altogether between 2 dishes very well then put it into the dish you intend to serve it in. Garnish your dish with slices of lemon and capers you may put in sturgon.

Elizabeth Ravell: 17th century
Suffolk/Essex border

Lines on Ipswich

A town without inhabitants, a river without water, streets without names, where asses wear boots.
Duke of Buckingham (1628-1687)

There is not any beggar asking alms in the whole place, a thing very extraordinary.
John Evelyn (1620-1706)

On the 19th I proceeded to Ipswich not imagining it to be the fine, populous and beautiful place that I found it to be.
William Cobbett, Rural Rides (1821-1832)

Gentlemen Farmers

It has been objected against me that my tenants live too much like gentlemen, driving their own curricles, perhaps, and drinking their port every day. I am proud to have such tenantry. We can all be clothed with imperial cloth of British growth, but I had rather that an Englishman's back should go without a superfine coat than that he should want plenty of wholesome mutton inside him.
Coke of Norfolk (1754-1842) at one of his famous sheep shearings at Holkham, after political opponents accused him of building palaces for farmhouses to curry favour with his tenants.

To Make Catchup

Take two quarts of the oldest strong beer you can get. Put to it one quart of red wine, ¾ of a pound of anchovies, 3 oz shallots peeled, ½ oz mace, the same of nutmeg, ¼ oz cloves, 3 large races (roots) of ginger cut in slices. Boil all together over a great fire until one third is wasted. The next day bottle it well for use. It will keep 7 years.
Martha Smith's book, Essex (1756)

Stuffing for a Turkey

Take a little Lemmon Time, Sweet margoram, suit, bread, salt, pepper, nutmeg, spice, the liver, temper it with an egg.
Martha Smith's book, Essex (1756)

Pudding for a Fish

Take a little Lemmon Time, Sweet Margrom, Lemmon Peeling, Salt, Pepper, Spice, Anchovy, Bread, Butter, mix it with an egg.
Martha Smith's book, Essex (1756)

Eighteenth Century Schooldays in Suffolk

His father resolved to give George the advantage of passing some time in a school at Bungay, on the borders of Norfolk, where it was hoped the activity of his mind would be disciplined into orderly diligence. I cannot say how soon this removal from the parental roof took place, but it must have been very early, as the following anecdote will show: The first night he spent at Bungay he retired to bed, he said, 'with a heavy heart, thinking of his fond indulgent mother'. But the morning brought a new misery. The slender and delicate child had hitherto been dressed by his mother. Seeing the other boys begin to dress themselves, poor George, in great confusion, whispered to his bedfellow, 'master G---, can you put on your shirt? - for - for I'm afraid I cannot'.

Soon after his arrival he had a very narrow escape. He and several of his schoolfellows were punished for playing at soldiers, by being put into a large dog-kennel, known by the terrible name of 'the black hole'. George was the first that entered, and the place being crammed full with offenders, the atmosphere soon became pestilentially close. The poor boy in vain shrieked that he was about to be suffocated. At last in despair, he bit the lad next to him violently in the hand. 'Crabbe is dying - Crabbe is dying,' roared the sufferer, and the sentinel at length opened the door, and allowed the boys to rush out into the air. My father said 'A minute more, and I must have died'.

The Life of George Crabbe by his Son

**George Crabbe, the poet-clergyman (1754-1832) was born at Aldeburgh, Suffolk. One brother became a successful glazier and then retired to Southwold. The next brother served in the Royal Navy, captained a Liverpool slave ship and married the owner's daughter, but died during an insurrection of the slaves. The fourth brother was also a seafarer imprisoned by the Spaniards and taken to Mexico where he prospered as a silversmith. He had to abandon his country, family, and property when persecuted as a Protestant, but was discovered in Honduras in 1803 by a sailor from Aldeburgh who gave him news of his famous brother George. After George's early schooldays in Bungay, he was sent to Mr Richard Haddon, a mathematician in Stowmarket, then apprenticed to a surgeon-apothecary in Wickhambrook at the age of 14, where he also had to do a considerable amount of work on the doctor's farm. He moved to another doctor's house at Woodbridge, and at the age of 20 was already an accomplished poet and began to educate himself in the classics and indulge in his passion for botany.

He moved to London and became a friend of the famous and a highly-regarded writer, but took orders in 1791 and returned to Aldeburgh as curate. He occupied a variety of livings in Suffolk and in the West Country, but his finest poetry was written about his birthplace.

Inebriety

Champagne the courtier drinks, the spleen to chase,
The colonel Burgundy, and Port his Grace.
Rev. George Crabbe (1775)

Rhubarb Jelly

Put your rhubarb into a brass pan with as much water as will keep it from burning, stew it to a pulp, strain it as for jelly, then add a pound of loaf sugar to each mutchkin of juice and boil till ready.
Elizabeth Garden, Redisham Hall, Suffolk (1847)

Almond Faggots

Half the white of an egg and ½ lb of sugar rubbed to an ice. ½ lb almonds laid on the white and dried on the fire. If you like them brown light an oven.
Elizabeth Garden, Redisham Hall, Suffolk (1847)

Sea Larks

You may stay yr stomack with little Pastys sometimes in Cold Mornings, for I doubt sea Larks will be too dear a Collation, and draw too much wine down.

Sir Thomas Browne (17th century Norwich physician, writing to his son)

Fat Man of Maldon

Mr Edward Bright, of Maldon in the County of Essex, who died at twenty-nine years of age, was an eminent shopkeeper of that town and supposed to be at that time, the largest man living, or that had ever lived in this island. He weighed six hundredweight, one quarter, and twenty-one pounds and stood about five feet nine inches high. His body was of an astonishing bulk, and his legs were as large as a middling man's body. Though of so great a weight and bulk, he was surprisingly active.

After Bright's death, a wager was proposed between Mr Codd and Mr Hants of Maldon, that five men at the age of twenty-one, then resident there, could not be buttoned within his waistcoat without breaking a stitch or straining a button. On the 1st of December, 1750, the wager was decided at the house of the widow Day, the Black Bull in Maldon, when five men and two more were buttoned within the waistcoat of the great personage deceased.

The Everyday Book

Boiled Cheese

4 oz of good mild rich English cheese, cut in thin slices, a piece of butter the size of **2** walnuts, two tablespoonsful of good cream. Put all into a stew pan and keep stirring till it boils and is quite smooth, then add the white and yolk of an egg. Stir it quickly, put into a dish and brown it before the fire. No cheese must be mixed that is old or with the blue mould. Dry toast is to be sent up with it.

Elizabeth Garden, Redisham Hall, Suffolk (1847)

R.S.V.P.

As sure as a bun
I'll be in at the fun;
For I'm the old Vicar
As sticks to his liquor;
And smokes a cigar,
Like a jolly Jack Tar:
I've no time for more,
For the Post's at the door:
But I'll be there by seven,
And stay 'till eleven,
For Boulge is my Heaven!

George Crabbe the Second replying to an invitation to Boulge Cottage from his friend, Woodbridge poet Edward FitzGerald

Home Made Yeast

Put 4 qts water into a pan with 2 oz of hops, let them boil ½ hour together, then stand till about the warmth of new milk. Add 1 lb flour, 1 lb sugar, 2 oz salt. Let it work 3 days in a covered vessel by the fire, stirring very frequently. 4th day add 3 lb finely mashed potatoes, let it stand till next day, then strain through a sieve and bottle in stone bottles, taking care not to cork it too tightly at first. Keep in a cool place or it will turn sour.

Elizabeth Garden, Redisham Hall, Suffolk (1847)

Transparent Puddings

Break the yolks of 6 eggs into a bowl, taking care no white adheres. Have ready to mix with these ¼ lb sifted sugar, ¼ lb fresh butter which have been previously warmed together in a jam pot to a honey (do not let them candy. Add this to the eggs and pour into 5 little tins or china moulds first placing in each a tea spoonful of marmalade. Place the moulds directly in a steamer and steam 20 mins. Take off - wait 5 minutes - turn out and serve.

Elizabeth Garden, Redisham Hall, Suffolk (1847)

Mary Doggett's Grandmother Pudding

Yolks of 6 eggs, 3 tablespoonfuls of lump sugar, 1 tablespoon of flour, a little nutmeg grated, 1 pint cream. Butter some cups and stick citron peel in them and serve with wine sauce. Bake 20 minutes.

Eliza Savory's receipt book, Norfolk (1859)

Mr Gann's Giblet Soup Most Excellent

One pair of Giblets cut in pieces about an inch long put them in a sauce pan with as much gravy or broth as will cover them or rather more, 3 onions sliced and a bunch of sweet herbs. Let them stew well together till almost done then strain the liquor from them and wash the giblets. Add to them a full gill of white wine and the gravy they were stewed in. Put a piece of butter in a stew pan over the fire and add as much flour as will make it a good thickness. Keep it stirring till it is a fine brown and add it to your soup. Season with pepper, salt and mace and squeeze in the juice of a lemon. Let them stew slowly till quite tender, be careful to keep them scumming quite clean. 2 eggs boiled hard the yolks broke and thrown into the tureen.

Elizabeth Garden, Redisham Hall, Suffolk (1847)

1891 Pumpkin Soup

Cut up the pumpkin into pieces about ½ inch square, removing the hard rind, about half the same quantity of potatoes. Place them in a saucepan with a piece of butter and a little salt. The saucepan should be about ¼ full. Put in also the tender green leaves of celery chopped fine (a handfull) and set to boil. In about 20 minutes or more the pumpkin and potatoes will be cooked. Add broth, and when boiling add 4 to 5 table spoonsful of washed rice. The rice will want from 20 to 30 minutes to cook. If the soup is too thick, add a small quantity of broth to make it thinner, and a little pepper.

Elizabeth Garden, Redisham Hall, Suffolk

Tribute to Jenny Lind

'Still harping on that Lindean wench! So is old Crabbe, who saw and heard her at Norwich, and for aught I know will carry her image enshrined in heart with him to the grave, if it be not quenched in those clouds of smoke he emits every night.'

Bernard Barton (Quaker banker and poet), 1847

**Jenny Lind, the Swedish Nightingale, and a celebrated Victorian singer, was commemorated in the name of the children's hospital in Norwich.*

A Fasting Condition

As early as five o'clock on Monday morning, hundreds of rustics poured into the town from different parts of the country; and by six, chaises, gigs, and vehicles of every description, some of which conveyed ten or twelve passengers, lined the several streets, until at length every stable and yard was full, as were also the inns and public-houses, so that adequate accommodation could not be afforded either to man or beast, and hundreds who had not been provident enough to bring food with them, were obliged to go to the place of execution in a fasting condition. The visitors consisted of almost every grade in society; but there was more labouring men than any other class: for although it was a fine harvest-day, the reapers &c. for miles around, 'struck' and came in gangs to witness the end of the murderer.

Among the concourse of visitors, were an extraordinary number from the vicinity of Polstead, who started from their respective places of abode at midnight. Boxford alone was said to supply near two hundred persons, and many came from places more distant than Norwich, Newmarket, or Cambridge.

Long before the hour arrived, every foot of ground was occupied in the spacious pasture, and the buildings and trees which stood within view of the scene of death had their occupants. In that part of the paddock near the road, grow a number of beautiful firs, and and other evergreens. Mr Orridge requested as a favour, that the spectators would not injure them, and owing to the universal respect which the public entertain for that gentleman, his request was strictly attended to.

Report of the execution of Wm. Corder at Bury St Edmunds for the murder of Maria Marten in the Red Barn, Polstead (1827)

Mrs Butcher's Syrup of Horehound

Take a large handful of horehound and boil it in a quart of water then strain it off to a pint, add a pint of either honey or treacle.

Mr James Wright's Receipt for Embrocation

6 oz olive oil (boiled) 2 oz aqua ammonia, 1 oz oil of turpentine, 2 drams origanum. Shake bottle well, rub in twice a day till tender.
Eliza Savory's receipt book, Norfolk (1859)

Drops for Diaarhia

Essence of peppermint, sal volatile, red lavender, equal parts. From 12-20 drops on a lump of sugar.
Eliza Savory's receipt book, Norfolk (1859)

Sustentacion of the Poor

There shalbe alwaies, God so contynuynge the charite & goodwyll of the people as there is at this present, fyvventene pore persons men & and women who shall have for their sustenstation and lyvinge, firste every weke, one busshell of wheate for to make breade, ij Busshelles of Malte for to make drynke & in redy monye for their meate two shillings and ijd Item every fortenight one pecke of Otemeale, & every monthe one pecke of salte And in the lent tyme syxe busshelles of pease For the Summer vj gallons of Butter and yearly vij hundred Fagottes of Wood.
Regulations for Saffron Walden (Essex) Almshouses (1549)

Medicine

1 oz turkey rhubarb, 1 oz epsom salts, 1 oz peppermint drops or 1d worth of the essence, ½ pint brandy, 1 pint of cold water. A wine glass full to be taken.
Eliza Savory's receipt book, Norfolk (1859)

Dinner at Yarmouth

He took a chop by the bone in one hand, and a potato in the other, and ate away with a very good appetite, to my extreme satisfaction. He afterwards took another chop, and another potato: and after that another chop and another potato. When he had done, he brought me a pudding, and having set it before me, seemed to ruminate, and to become absent in his mind for some moments.

'How's the pie?' he said, rousing himself.

'It's a pudding' I made answer.

'Pudding!' he exclaimed. 'Why, bless me, so it is! What!' looking at it, nearer. 'You don't mean to say it's a batter-pudding?'

'Yes, it is indeed.'

'Why, a batter-pudding,' he said, taking up a tablespoon, 'is my favourite pudding! Ain't that lucky? Come on, little 'un, and let's see who'll get most.'

The waiter certainly got most. He entreated me more than once to come in and win, but what with his tablespoon to my teaspoon, his dispatch to my dispatch, and his appetite to my appetite, I was left far behind at the first mouthful, and had no chance with him. I never saw anyone enjoy a pudding so much, I think; and he laughed when it was all gone, as if his enjoyment of it lasted still.

Charles Dickens: extract from David Copperfield

**Young David Copperfield was sent away to school for the first time and on the way the inexperienced little traveller had dinner at the Yarmouth coaching inn, where the wily coffee-room waiter took mean advantage of his innocence by drinking his ale and following it with most of David's meal.

The Midnight Steeplechase

On the breath of the blast
They are come - they are past -
Beating the ground
With a dead, dull sound,
As they speed on their midnight errand so fast;
The steam of their steeds,
Like a mist in the meads,
Veiled the moon in a curtain of cloud;
And the stars so bright
Shuddered in light,
As the unhallowed troop, in their shadowy shroud,
Galloping, whooping, and yelling aloud,
Fast and unfailing, and furious in flight,
Rattled on like the hailstorm, and vanished in night.

The Midnight Steeplechase from Ipswich barracks to Nacton Church (December 1803) commemorated in a set of four prints by Henry Alken

Fifteenth Century Valentine

My right well beloved Valentine, I recommend me unto you full heartily desiring to hear of your welfare which I beseech Almighty God to preserve unto his pleasure and your heart's desire. And if it please you to hear of my welfare I am not in good health of body nor of heart, nor shall I be until I hear from you. My mother hath laboured the matter to my father full diligently, but she can no more get that ye know of (his consent) but if ye love me as I trust verily that ye do, ye will not leave me therefore. If ye had not half the love-load that ye have, for to do the greatest labour that any woman in love might, I would not forsake you. My heart bids me evermore to love you truly, over all earthly thing...I beseech you that this bill be not seen of none earthly creature save only yourself.

Written by Marjorie Brews of the Manor House, Topcroft, Norfolk to her future husband, John Paston the younger (1477)

Syrup of Turneps (1791)

First bake your turneps in a pot with household bread and press out the liquor between two plates, then put a pint of this liquor to half a pint of hyssop and with as much brown suger candy as will sweeten it and boyle it to a syrop. It is good for a cold or consumption.

Elizabeth Ravell, Suffolk/Essex border

To Make a Surfit Water

Take a gallon of brandy, corn poppies a peck when the black bottoms are cut of, a pound of figs as many raisons, an ounce anny seed an ounce of coriander seeds, 2 ounces of liquorish, 2 ounces of scorzenero roots, 2 ounces single piony rotts (peony roots). Slice the rotts thin. Infuse these things fortnight or 3 weeks sturing them once only, then put them into a sif let it run through without pressing it must not run thick, then bottle it with lofe suger. Put these into your still with a laying of spere mint at the bottom and a laying of balme on the top, it will afford you near a quart of water.

Elizabeth Ravell: 17th century
Suffolk/Essex border
**Surfeit water was taken to aid the digestion when meals were often rich and heavy. A well-equipped household contained a still for the preparation of drinks and medicines.

Geography

Cromer crabs, Runton dabs,
Beeston babies, Sheringham ladies,
Weybourne witches, Salthouse ditches.
And the Blakeney people
Stand on the steeple,
And crack hazel-nuts
With a five-farthing beetle.
Blakeney bulldogs,
Morston Dodmen,
Binham bulls,
Stiffkey trolls,
Wells bitefinger.
Halvergate hares, Reedham rats,
Southwood swine and Cantley cats,
Acle asses, Moulton mules,
Beighton bears and Freethorpe fools.

Mrs Butcher's Mackerel Caviare

Cut six large mackerel without splitting into short round pieces. Mix 1 oz of beaten pepper, three large nutmegs, a little mace and a handful of salt. Stuff the pieces of mackerel with this stuffing in 3 or 4 places in each piece. Rub the pieces all over with it. Fry them brown with butter or oil, let them stand till cold, then put them in vinegar in a pot, cover the liquor with oil or fat, and they will keep eight months.

Eliza Savory's receipt book, Norfolk (1859)

Lines on Bury St Edmunds

A city more neatly seated the sun never saw, so curiously doth it hang upon a gentle descent; nor a monastery more noble, whether one considers the endowments, largeness or unparalleled magnificence.

John Leland (c 1506-1552) quoted by Camden

To conclude an account of Suffolk and not to sing the praises of Bury St Edmunds would offend every creature of Suffolk birth.

William Cobbett: Rural Rides (1821-32)

A handsome little town of thriving and cleanly appearance.

Charles Dickens: The Pickwick Papers

An Excellent Purge for Children or Old Persons (1791)

Take one spoonful of spirits of tartar prepared with sugar candy and rose water put it into a little broth and give it to either of them - it purges gently, comforts the heart and expels philegm and melancolly.

Elizabeth Ravell, Suffolk/Essex border

Widowers of Essex

All along this county it is very frequent to meet with Men that have had from Five or Six, to Fourteen or Fifteen Wives; and I was informed that in the Marshes, over against Candy Island, was a farmer who was then living with the five-and-twentieth; and that his Son, who was but Thirtyfive Years old, had already had about Fourteen…The reason was that they went into the Uplands for a Wife and when they took the young Women out of the wholesome fresh Air, they were clear and healthy; but when they came into the Marshes among the Fogs and Damps, they presently changed Complexion, got an Ague or two, and seldom held it above half a Year, or a Year at most.

Daniel Defoe: Tour Through Great Britain (1724)

Mrs Val Sheringham's Jeune Mange

1 oz of isinglass to a small ½ pint of boiling water, ¾ pint of sherry and a little brandy, six ozs of sugar, the juice and piece of lemon peel, the yolks of 4 eggs. Mix them well together. Stir them gently over the fire for about 20 minutes. Do not let it boil.

Eliza Savory's receipt book, Norfolk (1859)

Reconquest

Once a year the East country
Remembers its ancient master:
The fluid corn,
The grey-green swirling oats and luminous
                                                    barley
Brim up between banked hedges -
The strong tides join and sweep irresistibly over
Houses and telegraph poles
Till only the towered poplars and islanded
                                                    cathedrals,
Lincoln, Ely,
Look to the Pennines and High Germany.

R. N. Currey (1907-   )

The People of the Counties

They till the levels of the east,
Where blown grass borders the sea-strand,
And in the dunes for man and beast
They win their fodder. They make fat
The lean, themselves they profit least;
But this is not to wonder at.

Maurice Hewlett (1861-1923)

Mice in Peas

A piece of bitter alloes about the size of a nut. Put one pint boiling water on it. Stir till dissolved, let it stand till cold. This will soak about a qt of peas. Let them stand all night or a day and mice will not touch them.

Elizabeth Garden, Redisham Hall, Suffolk (1847)

Sallie's Clerical Biscuits

1 lb of flour, ¼ lb Butter rubbed into the flour, ½ lb of lump sugar and a large ½ spoonful of soda in warm milk (about a tea cup full). Add nutmeg, or essence of lemon or almonds. Mix into a stiff paste, let it lie an hour. Bake in a slow oven.

Eliza Savory's receipt book, Norfolk (1859)

Essex Air

The bleak, flat, sedgy shores of Essex shun,
Where fog perpetual veils the winter sun:
Though flattering Fortune there invite thy
                                                    stay,
Thy health the purchase of her smiles must
                                                    pay.

John Scott (1730-1783)

Small Gingerbread

½ lb butter, 1 lb coarse sugar, 2 oz ground ginger, 1 lb treacle, 1 lb of flour. Treacle and butter to be poured hot over other things. Roll out and bake on tins.

Eliza Savory's receipt book, Norfolk (1859)

Peggy Muns Stiffkey Cakes

4 teacups of flour, 1 oz butter, 1 oz sugar, 20 drops of flavouring, 1 teaspoonful baking powder. Make up with eggs, cut out in thick cakes.

Julia R. Spurrell, Pudding Norton Hall, Norfolk (1865)

Kitchen Pepper

Mix in the finest powder 1 oz ginger; cinnamon, black pepper, nutmeg and jamaica pepper (allspice) ½ oz each, ten cloves and teaspoon of salt.

Julia R. Spurrell, Pudding Norton Hall, Norfolk (1865)

To Pot Cheese

Take 3 lbs of cheese, ½ lb butter, ½ oz mace and a gill fo white wine. Beat them well in a mortar till quite smooth, then put it close in a jar. When hard, cover with clarified butter and set in a cool place.

Julia R. Spurrell, Pudding Norton Hall, Norfolk (1865)

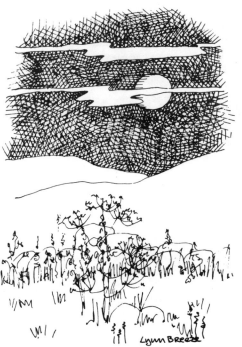

A Lament for Walsingham

Bitter, bitter, oh! to behould
    the grasse to growe
Where the walls of Walsingham
    So statly did shewe.
Such were the workes of Walsingham
    while shee did stand!
Such are the wrackes as now do shewe
    of that holy-land!
Levell, levell, with the ground
    the towres do lie,
Which with their golden glittering tops
    pearsed once to the skye!
Wher weare gates, no gates ar now;
    the waies unknowen,
Wher the presse of peares did passe,
    while her fame far was blowen,
Oules do scrike wher the sweetest himnes
    lately were songe;
Toades and serpentes hold their dennes
    where the Palmers did thronge.

Anon (16th century)

Baking Powder

½ lb ground rice, ¼ lb carbonate of soda, 2 oz tartaric acid to be well mixed.

Julia R.Spurrell, Pudding Norton Hall, Norfolk (1865)

Elizabethan Drinks

There is a kind of swish-swash made also in Essex, and divers other places, with honeycombs and water, which the homely country wives, putting some pepper and a little other spice among, call mead, very good in mine opinion for such as love to be loose bodied at large, or a little eased of the cough. Otherwise it differeth so much from the true metheglin as chalk from cheese. Truly it is nothing else but the washing of the combs, when the honey is wrung out, and one of the best things that I know belonging thereto is that they spend but little labour, and less cost in making of the same, and therefore no great loss if it were never occupied.

William Harrison (Rector of Radwinter, Essex): Description of England (1577)

Doctor's Prescription

Fro ye first day to ye 9 as much as
    will ly upon a groat.
Fro ye 9 day to ye 11 as much as
    will ly upon a sixpence.
Fro ye 11 day to ye 25 as much as
    will ly upon a shilling.
Fro ye 25 day to ye 32 as much as
    will ly upon a sixpence.
Fro ye 32 day to ye 36 as much as
    will ly upon a groat.

Elizabeth Ravell: 17th century Suffolk/Essex border

Dinners for a Parson

January 28th, 1780
We had for dinner a Calf's Head, boiled Fowl and Tongue, a Saddle of Mutton rosted on the side table, and a fine Swan rosted with Currant Jelly Sauce for the first course. The second course a couple of Wild Fowl, called Dun Fowls, Larks, Blamange, Tarts, etc., etc., and a good desert of Fruit after, amongst which was a Damson Cheese. I never eat a bit of a Swan before, and I think it good eating with sweet sauce. The Swan was killed three weeks before it was eat and yet not the least bad taste in it.

May 14th, 1789
We had for dinner some boiled Tench, Eels, fryed, etc., all which Mrs Custance sent us last night after their return home which was very, very kind indeed of them. We also had for dinner a boiled knuckle of Veal and Pigg's Face, a Fore-quarter of Lamb rosted, and a Plumb Pudding; four nice spring chicken rosted and Asparagus, green Apricot tarts and custards; Colliflower, Brocoli, Spinage, Cucumbers and a large bowl of Sallading. The company left us a little before 8 o'clock.

James Woodforde (Rector of Weston Longville, Norfolk): The Diary of a Country Parson

Eleventh Century Labour Troubles

I love you, and I am striving to deliver you, slow and indolent as you are, out of the hands of the divine severity. Often have I stirred you up in person by reminding you both privately and publicly of your duty in this respect, to apply yourselves fervently and diligently to the work of your church, and to show carefulness in that work, as done under the inspection of God's own eyes. I was wont to entreat and to persuade you and would that I had succeeded in convincing your minds how great is the sincerity with which God must be served. But alas! The work drags on, and in providing materials you show no enthusiasm. Behold the servants of the King and mine own are really earnest in the works allotted to them. They gather stones, carry them to the spot and fill with them fields and ways, houses and courts. You meanwhile are asleep with folded hands, numbed, as it were, and frost-bitten by a winter of negligence, shuffling and failing in your duty through a paltry love of ease.

Letter from Bishop Losinga to the monks building Norwich Cathedral (11th century)

Eliza Butcher's Raspberry Cream

Take some raspberry jam, cream, juice of a lemon and sugar to taste. Whisk all well together until quite stiff.

Eliza Savory's receipt book, Norfolk (1859)

Mrs Cook's Deepdale Sponge Cakes

7 eggs leaving out 2 whites, ¾ lb loaf sugar, ¼ pint of boiling water poured on the sugar. Poured hot over the eggs and stirring them at the same time. Beat 10 minutes, add ½ lb of flour. Mix it in and put in the pan and bake.

Eliza Savory's receipt book, Norfolk (1859)

Mrs Butcher's Receipt for the Eggs

Boil hard in the shells, peel them and put into a jar with a little mace, cloves and whole pepper. Boil Vinegar enough to cover them and pour over hot. Stand two days, again scald the vinegar and tie down.

Eliza Savory's receipt book, Norfolk (1859)

Very Good Water for a Cough or Stuffing in 'ye Stomack

Take six pints of milk of a red cow, and put to it hysope, and balme, foalsfoot and liver-wort of each 2 handfulls, of parsely roots, fennell roots, pith'd slic'd and cut somewhat small and lungwort of each one handfull, a pound of raisons of ye sun stoned and as many figgs sliced thinn and bruised, half a pound of liqqurish scraped, sliced thinn and bruised and a qr of a pound of annise seeds bruised. Steep all those a night and in ye morning betimes still them in an ordinary still untill they begin to grow fome which dry; it will yeild a bottel or five pints of water so as you keep a moderate fire you shall do well to mix ye water for ye first will be stronger than ye last. You may fire it in a warm oven, it will keep ye better. You can only make it att spring and at Michaelmas time. Probatum est.

Elizabeth Ravell: 17th century Suffolk/Essex border

Philosophy

The world is my country;
Every man is my brother;
To do good is my religion.

Thomas Paine of Thetford (1737-1809)

Cough Mixture

2 table spoonfuls of honey, 2 ditto treacle, 3 ditto vinegar, 20 drops of peppermint, 20 drops of laudanum, all gently simmered together.

Julia R. Spurrell, Pudding Norton Hall, Norfolk (1865)

Black Draught

1 oz Epsom salts, 1d senna, 1½d black liquorice. Simmer slowly the senna and liquorice in ¾ pint of water and strain over the salt.

Julia R. Spurrell, Pudding Norton Hall, Norfolk (1865)

Epilepsy

Bromide of potassium in doses of 5 to 10 grains.

Julia R. Spurrell, Pudding Norton Hall, Norfolk (1865)

Rheumatism

Dissolve ½ oz camphor in a pt of spirits of turpentine and rub on the part affected night and morning - a perfect cure.

Julia R. Spurrell, Pudding Norton Hall, Norfolk (1865)

Elizabethan Feasts

At such times as the merchants do make their ordinary or voluntary feasts, it is a world to see what great provision is made of all manner of delicate meats, from every quarter of the country, wherein, beside that they are often comparable to the nobility of the land, they will seldom regard anything that the butcher usually killeth, but reject the same as not worthy to come in place. In such cases also gellifs of all colours, mixed with a variety in the representation of sundry flowers, herbs, trees, forms of beasts, fish, fowls and fruits, and thereunto marchpane wrought with no small curiosity, tarts of divers hues, and sundry denominations, conserves of old fruits, foreign and home-bred, suckets, codinacs, marmalades, marchpane, sugarbread, gingerbread, florentines, wild-fowl, venison of all sorts, and sundry outlandish confections, altogether seasoned with sugar, do generally bear the sway, besides infinite devices of our own not possible for me to remember. Of the potato, and such venerous roots as are brought out of Spain, Portugal and the Indies to furnish up our banquets, I speak not.

William Harrison (Rector of Radwinter, Essex): Description of England (1577)

I'm a Shrimp! I'm a Shrimp

I'm a shrimp! I'm a shrimp! Of diminutive size
Inspect my antennæ, and look at my eyes;
I'm a natural syphon, when dipped in a cup,
For I drain the contents to the latest drop up.
I care not for craw-fish, I heed not the prawn,
From a flavour especial my fame has been drawn;
No e'en to the crab or the lobster to yield,
When I'm properly cooked and efficiently peeled.
Quick! Quick! Pile the coals - let your saucepan be deep,
For the weather is warm, and I'm sure not to keep.
Off, off with my head - split my shell into three-
I'm a shrimp! I'm a shrimp! - to be eaten with tea.

Robert Brough

To Make a Medison for the Canker in the Mouth

Take 1 ounce of lemon ginger on ounce of long pepper beten small searced, 1 spoonfull of honey, 1 spoonfull of venice treakel, half a quarter of an ounce of cloves beaten and searsed. Put to this half a quarter of a pint of whit wine veniger and as much brandy boyl them till it be thick.

Elizabeth Ravell: 17th century
Suffolk/Essex border
**Venice was the main centre of treacle production, supplying most of western Europe, but in the 15th century Genoa treacle and Flanders treacle became better known in England.

For a Cough

Take a qr of a pound of raisons of ye sun boyle ym very well yn take away ye stones and skins, yn take ye pulp and beat it very well adding to it 2 ounces of conserve of red roses 2 pennyworth of syrrop of coltsfood, one pennyworth of syrrop of poppy two ounces of brown sugar candy and when you have beaten all these well together add to it six drops of spirit of vitrioll - Let it be taken morning and evening on the point of a knife.

Elizabeth Ravell: 17th century
Suffolk/Essex border

Unlucky Black Cat

This informant saith That on Tuesday last being the - daye of August last hee was cominge from Elsenham to Teakly in the Countie of Essex, and this informant saith that his fathers dogge was with him, and the dogge did runne after a hogge which was John Dishes hogge of Teakly aforesaid, and that Hellen ye wife of the said John seeinge the dogge to runne after her hogge as aforesaid, did thereupon threaten this informant and told this informant hee had as good not to have suffred his dogge to have worried her hogge, for hee should have noe great joy after it. And this informant saith that ever since Saturday morninge laste, beinge the third of September instant, hee hath had exceedinge stronge & many painfull fittes to ceize on him att severall times, and that his fittes doth hold him halfe an howre or thereaboutes. And this informant saith that yesterday morninge there came a thinge uppon his bedd, like a blacke catt, and this morninge there came another thinge like a hedgehogge and satt uppon a sticke neere this informantes bedd side (hee beinge in bedd) and immediately after the sight of those thinges, his fittes ceized on him very stronge and painfull, and he saith hee feeleth some thinge runne uppe into his body whilest it comes to his throate and then hee is almost strangled & is in great torture paine and misery.

The informacion of Rewben Bowier late of Wicken Brooke in the Countie of Suffolk singleman taken uppon oath before Christopher Muschampe Esquire one of the Justices of the Peace for the Countie of Essex the 5th daye of September, 1653.

To Make a Green Oyntment for Kibe Hel (Chapped Heels)

Take sheeps dung new made and boyl in it a like quantity of mutton suit half an hour then strain it out and keep it for use. When you use it wash the plase with a little butter and bere then spread a plaister and lay it on, it will hele it in once or twice.

Elizabeth Ravell: 17th century Suffolk/Essex border

Hard Cheese

A cantle of Essex cheese
Was well a foot thick
Full of maggots quick;
It was huge and great
And Mightly strong meat
For the devil to eat,
It was tart and punicate.

John Skelton

**Skelton, Rector of Diss, Norfolk, was a poet and tutor to Henry VIII, and described himself as 'Rector of Hell'. Diss was also famous for Diss Bread, a kind of gingerbread reputedly soothing to those with a hangover.

The Mayor's Feast in Norwich 1561

The Mayor's share of the expense was one pound twelve shillings and ninepence; the feast-makers, four in number, paying the rest. The Mayor's bill of fare was as follows:

Eight stone of beef, at 8d a stone and a sirloin	0	5	8
Two collars of brawn	0	1	0
Four cheeses, at 4d a cheese	0	1	4
Eight pints of butter	0	1	6
A hinder quarter of veal	0	0	10
A leg of mutton	0	0	5
A fore quarter of veal	0	0	5
Loin of mutton and shoulder of veal	0	0	9
Breast and coat of mutton	0	0	7
Six pullets	0	1	0
Four couple of rabbits	0	1	8
Four brace of partridges	0	2	0
Two Guinea cocks	0	1	6
Two couple of mallards	0	1	0
Thirty-four eggs	0	0	6
Bushel of flour	0	0	6
Peck of oatmeal	0	0	2
Sixteen white bread loaves	0	0	4
Eighteen loaves of white wheat bread	0	0	9
Three loaves of Meslin bread	0	0	3
Nutmegs, mace, cinnamon and cloves	0	0	3
Four pounds of Barbary sugar	0	1	0
Sixteen oranges	0	0	2
A barrel of double strong beer	0	2	6
A barrel of table beer	0	1	0
A quarter of wood	0	2	2
Two gallons of white wine and canary	0	2	0
Fruit, almonds, sweetwater, perfumes	0	0	4
The cook's wages	0	1	2
Total	1	12	9

Sandringham Jelly

Dissolve ½ oz gelatine in 1 pint of milk, ½ lb lump sugar and the peel of one lemon. When it boils, pour it through a sieve on 3 well-beaten eggs, stirring all the time. When cool, add the juice of 2 lemons. Reserve a little of the milk to mix with the eggs before pouring on the boiling milk.

Household recipe book, Norfolk (early 20th century)

Everingtons Sloe Gin

1 gallon gin, 2½ lbs loaf sugar, 1½ oz of bitter almonds (divided), 5 pints ripe sloes. Put in a 2 gallon bottle well corked. Shake the bottle once a week for three months, strain off and bottle.

Household recipe book, Norfolk (early 20th century)

Mrs Sheringham's Citron Puddings

Mix a spoonful of flour with the yolks of 4 eggs, a little nutmeg. Warm ½ pint of thick sweet cream and 2 ozs of candied citron peel cut very thin. Bake in tea cups 20 minutes or ½ hour, and serve turned out with wine sauce.

Eliza Savory's receipt book, Norfolk (1859)

Solid Syllabub

A pint of thin cream, one and half oz of Isinglass, ½ lb of loaf sugar, a piece of lemon peel boiled together 20 minutes, then strain them. When cold and it begins to thicken, add a pint of white wine, a glass of brandy and the juice of a lemon. Stir it well together and put into a shape.

Eliza Savory's receipt book, Norfolk (1859)

Weasenham Hall Mincemeat (1914)

3 lbs currants, 3 lbs raisins, 3 lbs suet, 2 lbs moist sugar, ½ lb mixed candied peel, 6 lemons boiled whole till tender in two waters, ½ pint brandy, 2 glasses of sherry, 2 dozen cloves, 2 nutmegs and a little allspice.

Household recipe book, Norfolk (early 20th century)

Mrs Ranson's Powder Plum Cake

1¼ lb of flour, 6 oz of butter, 6 oz of sugar, 2 eggs well beaten, ½ lb of currants, candied peel, a teaspoonful of baking powder dissolved in ¼ pint of new milk.

Eliza Savory's receipt book, Norfolk (1859)

The Norfolk Bittern

The *Ardea stellaris botaurus* or bitour (bittern) is also common and esteemed the better dish. In the belly I found a frog in a hard frost at Christmas. Another I kept in a garden 2 years feeding it with fish, mice and frogges, in defect whereof making a scrape for sparrows and small birds, the bitour made shift to maintaine herself upon them.

Sir Thomas Browne: Notes on Certain Birds Found in Norfolk (1664)

**The bittern, famous for its loud booming cry, ceased to breed in Norfolk in 1869, but in 1911, it was proved to have bred again in the county. It was a popular bird in the Middle Ages, and features in the poetry of Chaucer and Skelton, as well as being noted by later writers such as Dryden, Drayton, Crabbe, Burns, Wordsworth and Southey.

Baking Day

On a baking day, the bread used to be laid in the putch, and put to rise. When you baked a big batch to last a week, it took a long time before it was ready for the oven, especially if the yeast was not fresh. We had to make our bread with brewer's yeast in those days. I used to fetch it. Our mothers used to say, 'Don't you bring me Porter yeast, do you can take it back.' No gas ovens or cooking ranges in those days. If there were any ranges at all, they were in the tradesmen's houses, who paid for them in their rent. Our ovens were of brick. You had to heat them with bush faggots, and have a long pole to stir the ashes about. When you saw the bricks were white all over, you knew you had got a nice oven for your bread, for that was what the ovens mostly contained. There were not many cakes and pies. Sometimes we had a pumking pie in winter, but that was a luxury. I have heard the old ladies say they were more tired after baking than if they had stood at the wash tub for two days.

Mrs Scarfe Webb (aged 70) writing in East Anglian Magazine (1946)

The Mistletoe Bough

Full fifty years were past, and all forgot,
When on an idle day, a day of search
Mid the old lumber in the gallery,
A mouldering chest was noticed; and 'twas
said:
'Why not remove it from its lurking place?'
'Twas done as soon as said; but on the way
It burst, it fell; and lo, a skeleton
With here and there a pearl, an emerald
stone.
All else had perished - save a nuptial ring.
There, then, had she found a grave!
Within that chest had she concealed herself,
Fluttering with joy, the happiest of the
happy;
When a spring-lock, that lay in ambush
there,
Fastened her down for ever!

Part of the legend of The Mistletoe Bough, telling the story of the Christmas Day wedding of Agnes de Clifford to Lord Lovell of Lovell's Hall, Terrington St Clement. After the banquet, a game of hide-and-seek was played, and the young bride climbed into a spring-locked chest which concealed her body for 50 years.

Mackerel Fishing

The mackerel fishery employs fifty vessels of from twenty to forty tons, carrying nine or ten men and a boy. Each boat has twelve score nets, each twenty yards on the lint, seventeen yards on the rope, and four yards in depth. It has fifteen warps, value £6 each; the value of the nets being £15 per score. The fishery begins on May 4th and ends July 8th, the fishing ground being ten leagues from Yarmouth, east north-east. The catch is brought in every morning, the fish sold for the London market being transhipped without landing to small vessels, except early in the season when it is dispatched in carts. The average catch per boat weekly is about £25, the value per hundred varying from three guineas to ten shillings. The men employed are all adventurers, their wages very low, their chief profit that of the venture. The mackerel fishery is on the increase, but its chief advantage is the keeping men employed before the herring season commences. Mackerel boats run to London in from twenty to thirty hours.

Report of Mr Stephen Godfrey of Yarmouth (1785)

Words of Wisdom

Good broth and good keeping do much, now and than,
Good diet with wisdom, best comforteth man.

When fish is scant and fruit of trees,
supply that want, with butter and cheese.
But huswives, that learne not to make their own cheese;
with trusting of others, have this for their feese.
Their milke slapt in corners their creame al to soat;
their milke pannes so slotte that their cheeses belost.

Conserves of barberry, quinces and such,
with sirops, that easeth the sickly so much.
Good peason and leekes, to make poredge in Lent
and peascods in July, save fish to be spent.

Thomas Tusser (1557)
***Tusser, the farmer-poet of Rivenhall (Essex) set out wise maxims for the farmer and housewife in 'Five Hundred Pointes of Good Husbandrie'.**

A Traveller's Breakfast

A noble breakfast. There was tea and coffee, a goodly white loaf and butter, there were a couple of eggs and two mutton chops - there was boiled and pickled salmon - fried trout...also potted trout and potted shrimps.

A few weeks later

What a breakfast! Pot of hare; ditto of trout; pot of prepared shrimps; dish of plain shrimps; tin of sardines; beautiful beefsteak; eggs, muffins, large loaf, and butter, not fogetting capital tea.

George Borrow
***George Borrow, of Dereham (Norfolk), was famous for his travels in the middle of the 19th century, described in 'Romany Rye,' 'Lavengro 'and 'Wild Wales.'**

Furniture Oil

1 pt linseed oil, 1 oz button of antimony, 1 oz sulphuric acid, ½ oz loaf sugar, ½ pint vinegar. Mix these well together and shake before using. Put a small quantity on the furniture and rub with a piece of flannel. Polish with soft dry rags.

Julia R. Spurrell, Pudding Norton Hall, Norfolk (1865)

Village Concert at Thaxted

Mrs Potton is the next performer. From my peephole in the back curtain I can't quite see her as she walks on, but the cheering and stamping surprise me considerably. I had not believed her to be so popular. And then the reason became apparent. Ample of architecture, and florid of hue, she struts the stage in an extravagant paraphrase of bull-fighting attire. Black satin breeches caress her ample thighs, a scarlet cummerbund and yellow blouse delineate her convexity all too unkindly, a broad black felt crowns saucily her coal black curls, and behind the left ear lurks a paper rose. I am deprived of half the effect, but if the front view is anything like as funny as the rear she is doing pretty well. Presently, by much waving of an over-diamonded hand, she achieves silence, and explains with a kind of pained resignation that she isn't funny at all. She is a bull-fighter who loves a little gypsy, and is going to sing a song about it. Whereat, with slightly too much ambition, sublime courage, a harsh soprano, and very little justification, she plunges into 'The Toreador's Song' from *Carmen*.

Ethelind Fearon: Most Happy Husband (1946)

Aldeburgh

There, fed by Food they love, to rankest size,
Around the dwellings Docks and Wormwood
rise;
Here the strong Mallow strikes her slimy Root,
Here the dull Nightshade hangs her deadly
Fruit;
On hills of Dust the Henbane's faded green,
And pencill'd Flower of sickly scent is seen:
At the Wall's base the fiery Nettle springs,
With Fruit globose and fierce with poison'd
Stings;
Above (the Growth of many a Year) is spread
The yellow level of the Stone-crop's Bed;
In every Chink delights the Fern to grow,
With glossy Leaf and tawny Bloom below:
These, with our sea-weed, rolling up and down,
Form the contracted Flora of the Town.

Extract from The Borough: George Crabbe (1754-1832)

To Wash Oil Cloth

Never scrub it. Wash with large soft cloth and lukewarm or cold water. On no account use soap or water hot. When dry, sponge it with milk and wipe with a soft dry cloth. Never buy one made within the year.

Elizabeth Garden, Redisham Hall, Suffolk (1847)

To Wash Lace

Cover a bottle, the larger the better, with a linen case made to fit tight. Roll the lace round it, taking care that the edge is kept smooth and that the head of the succeeding round covers it, tack the lace, if there are several lengths in the slightest possible manner and without any knots. When the lace is all rolled around the bottle, cover it tight with linen. Then rub it well with soap (the best cured) or if very dirty make a strong lather and let the bottle remain in it for a night. Rinse well by pouring water over it. If possible, expose the bottle to the sun, watering it frequently, and also to the night air, and let it dry thoroughly before you open it. Avoid hot water - it destroys the look of newness.

Elizabeth Garden, Redisham Hall, Suffolk (1847)

Fred Jay's Pomade

1 oz white wax, 2 oz spermacetti, 2 oz castor oil, 12 oz olive oil, ½ oz palm oil, 2 drams oil of lemon, 1 dram bergamot, ½ dram cloves, 12 drops cassia, 20 drops tincture of cantharides. Melt the wax and spermacetti, then add the oils and scents.

Julia R. Spurrell, Pudding Norton Hall, Norfolk (1865)

To Preserve Cut Flowers

Sprinkle them lightly with fresh water, then put the bouquet into a vessel containing soap suds. Take them out every morning and lay the bouquet sideways (the stick entering first) into clean water. Keep it there a minute or two then take it out and sprinkle the flowers lightly by hand with water. Replace it in the suds and it will bloom as fresh as when gathered. Change the soap-suds every 3 or 4 days. By this means, a bouquet can be kept fresh a month.

Elizabeth Garden, Redisham Hall, Suffolk (1847)

Grotesque Exploits

A suspension bridge was built in 1821 at the north end of Yarmouth at a cost of £4000; but on May 2, 1845, gave way with fatal results. A large crowd had imprudently assembled upon it to witness the grotesque exploits of a clown of a travelling circus who promised to pass by in a tub drawn by geese. Four hundred persons were precipitated into the water, and seventy-nine were drowned.

M. E. C. Walcott: The East Coast of England (1861)

Directions for a Lady's Hood

Cast on 70 stitches
Knit 50 needles red wool
Knit 18 needles white
Knit 28 needles red
Knit 64 needles white which form the lining

Curtain

Cast on 70 stitches
Knit 34 needles red; increase a stitch each needle till you have 104 stitches. Knit 18 needles white.
Knit 28 needles red.
Knit 56 needles white for lining.
In the last 34 needles decrease a stitch each needle till you have 70 again.

A needle is ½ a row.

Elizabeth Garden, Redisham Hall, Suffolk (1847)

Mrs Waters' Pickled Lemons

Boil the lemons two or three times in water until soft and not bitter, then cut in slices and take out the pips. Boil some vinegar with spice and when cold pour over the lemons.

Julia R. Spurrell, Pudding Norton Hall, Norfolk (1865)

Lines on Yarmouth

If anyone has a grudge against any particular insurance company, the best way to gratify it would be to buy a heavy life annuity and then retire to Yarmouth.

Charles Dickens

Yarmouth is the most uncomfortable place in the nation for a man of learning to be fix'd in, the people being a most illiberal, tarpaulin crew.

Memoirs of a Royal Chaplain (1729-1761)

I do not see that the ladies here come behind any of the neighbouring counties either in breeding, beauty or behaviour…and they generally go beyond them in fortunes.

Daniel Defoe: Tour Through the Eastern Counties (1722)

Milk Punch

1 quart rum, 1 quart of water that has been boiled, ½ pint new milk, ¾ lb powdered lump sugar and ½ pt lemon juice. Add the peels of six lemons and grated nutmeg and after standing some hours, strain it through a jelly bag until it looks bright. Bottle it and keep for use well corked.

Julia R. Spurrell, Pudding Norton Hall, Norfolk (1865)

Aldeburgh

There poppies nodding, mock the hope of
toil;
There the blue bugloss paints the sterile soil;
Hardy and high, above the slender sheaf,
The slimy mallow waves her silky leaf;
O'er the young shoot the charlock throws a
shade,
And clasping tares cling round the sickly
blade;
With mingled tints the rocky coast abound,
And a sad splendour vainly shines around.
*Extract from The Village: George Crabbe
(1754-1832)*

Mrs Parker's Pigeon Jelly

Have ready a savory jelly and with it half fill
the bowl you wish to shape it in. Roast the
bird as if sitting up and when cold put a
spray of myrtle in its mouth. When the jelly
and the birds are cold (see that no gravy
hangs to the birds) lay them upside down in
the jelly. Before the rest gets cold, pour it
over about an inch above the birds' feet. This
should be done the day before wanted.
*Julia R. Spurrell, Pudding Norton Hall,
Norfolk (1865)*

Mrs Parker's Plum Sauce for Roast Pig

Put a round of stale bread cut thick into as
much cold water as will boil it thick. Add ¼ lb
currants when the water is cold. Let them be
nicely plumped, sweeten it to your taste and
add 1 wineglass of sherry and 2 of brandy. Stir
with a fork 1 hour before wanted.
*Julia R. Spurrell, Pudding Norton Hall, Norfolk
(1865)*

To Make Yeast

Boil 1 lb of good flour and ¼ lb brown sugar
and a little salt in two gallons of water for an
hour. When milk warm, bottle it and cork it
close. It will be fit to use in 24 hours. One pint
of this will be sufficient for 18 lbs of bread.
*Household recipe book, Norfolk (early 20th
century)*

Return to England

I will go back down that Ipswich-Sudbury road again, go down it slowly some day, and look for my old friends. The girls at the window at Boxford will not be there, the convalescent soldiers of Hintlesham will be gone, there will be no German bomber streaking down the road, and the old bearded man will have gone to his long home. But the rolling fields, and the bright yellow straw stacks, the empty streets of Hadleigh and the ancient thatched cottages will be there and lovely lapwings will wheel over the fallow fields and I shall almost feel at home, and among old friends again. For here we are close to the heart of England.

Bob Arbib (American Staff Sergeant who spent two years of 1939-45 War as a surveyor in Suffolk, and wrote a book on his life in England): 'Here We Are Together".

Carnations

THE SONS of FLORA will hold their Annual Feast at the Maid's Head in St Simon's in Norwich, on Wednesday the 6th of August next; where all Gentlemen, who are Admirers of the Beauties of Nature, are desired to come and view the greatest Variety of New and Well-blown CARNATIONS that the Year produces. N.B. There will be a VENISON FEAST, and Stewards are provided for the ensuing Year.

Advertisement in Norwich Mercury (1746)

The Lady Chesterfield Walnut Water

Take a pound of herb grace and a pound of green walnuts husks and all and on pound of green figs, bruse the walnuts in a stoon morter by them reduse then brush the herb grace at the bottom then a laying of walnuts and then of figs and so do till all is in the still then still it as you do other waters. The vertue of this water it is food for any that are ill at thire stomack or a feavour, on may take it that is ill with child tow spoonfulls at night when they go to bed or at any other time in a feavour take 3 spoonfulls warm in the morning and sweet after it but if the party be disperately ill then mix as much mearydate (mithridate) as a little nut with it and so take it in the morning fasting and sweet after it, if they dosn mend give them one like quantity at night without merrydate.

Elizabeth Ravell: 17th century
Suffolk/Essex border

Sir Thomas

A good soft pillow for that good white head
Were better than a churlish turf of France.

Lines from Shakespeare spoken by Henry V before the Battle of Agincourt to Sir Thomas Erpingham, whose name is commemorated by a Norfolk village, and by the Erpingham Gate in Norwich.

Pot Pourri

Put into a large china jar the following ingredients in layers with bay salt strewed between. Two pecks of damask roses part in buds and part blown, violets and orange flowers and jasmine, a handful of each. Orris root sliced, benjamin and storax, two ounces of each. A quarter of an ounce of musk, a quarter of a pound of angelica roots sliced, a quarter of the red parts of clove gillaflowers, two handfuls of lavender flowers, half a handful of rosemary leaves and flowers, bay and laurel leaves half a handful of each, three Seville oranges stuck as full of cloves as possible, dried in a cool room, and pounded and covered down.

Eliza Savory's receipt book, Norfolk (1859)

Stomach Tincture

Geniacum Shavings 4 ozs
Senna Leaves 4 ozs
Yellow Campanula Root 4 ozs
Liquorish Root 4 ozs
Coriander Seed 4 ozs
Fennel Seed 2 ozs
Raisins picked from the Stalk 8 ozs
Spirits of Aniseed 12 Pints to be infused with gentle heat for 12 days, strain it through a fine sieve. Return the Ingredients into the Vessel and add 2 Quarts more spirits of Aniseed to be infused for 6 Days more and drawn again.

Mrs Tuffnell, Langleys, Gt. Waltham, Essex (1815)

To Make Aqua Mirabilis (Miracle Water)

Take cubebs, gallingale, cardames, milk of flowers, cinnamon of each one dram brused small, juice of celandine one pin, juce of speremint half a pint, juce of balm half a pint, suger on pound, flowers of peagles (cowslips) rosemary, borage bugloss marrigolds of each tow drams, the best sack 3 pints, strong angilio water on pint. Bruse the spices and soke them in the sack and juces one night. The next morning still it in an ordinary or glass still, lay some hearts tongue leaves in the bottom of the still. The vertue of this water it preserve the lungs without grievances and helpeth them being grieved, it suffereth not the blood to pietrifye but multiplieth the same, it suffereth not the heart to burn.

Elizabeth Ravell: 17th century
Suffolk/Essex border

Medical Bill

Strengthening mixture	2/6
The Pectoral mixture	2/-
Reducing a Fracture on the Arm	£1.1.0

Dr Clarance, Thaxted, Essex (1775)

 **It is interesting to note the high cost of medical treatment in the days of low wages. What happened to a farm labourer who broke his arm?*

Here be Dragons

The Cockatrice of Saffron Walden took up residence near that pleasant Essex town in the Middle Ages. It broke stones and blasted trees with its breath. It burned everything it passed over, and, by merely looking at them, killed so many of the inhabitants of Saffron Walden that the town was in danger of being depopulated. It was finally destroyed by an intrepid warrior encased in a specially constructed armour of crystal glass.

Saffron Walden appears to have been a regular hot-bed of these peculiar types of vermin. In 1669, the town and district were afflicted by a flying serpent, some nine feet long and as thick as a stout man's thigh. Its eyes were lustrous and its teeth were white and sharp. Its appearance is vouched for in a document signed by the Churchwardens, Constable, Overseer for the Poor and four prominent householders, of which there is a copy in the library of the British Museum.

The East Anglian Magazine, 1946

Miss Rice's Way With A Strain

1 quart of Vinegar 4 ounces of Salt Petre 3 ounces of Oil of Turpentine.

Elizabeth Hicks, Suffolk/Essex border (late 18th century)

Playford

Upon a hill-side green and fair
The happy traveller sees
White cottages peep here and there
Between the tufts of trees;
With a white farmhouse on the brow,
And an old grey Hall below
With moat and garden found;
And on a Sabbath wandering near
Through all the quiet place you hear
A Sabbath breathing sound
Of the church-bell slowly swinging
In an old grey tower above
The wooded hill, where birds are singing
In the deep quiet of the grove;
And when the bell shall cease to ring,
And the birds no longer sing,
And the grasshopper is heard no more
A sound of praise, of prayer,
Rises along the air,
Like the sea murmur from a distant shore.

Bernard Barton (1784-1849)

For a Sprain

Put the white of an egg in a saucer and beat it up with a lump of alum till it becomes a curd, then rub the sprain with it (an opera dancer's receipt).

Elizabeth Garden, Redisham Hall, Suffolk (1847)

Weasenham Cakes

½ lb finely powdered lump sugar, ½ lb butter, ¾ lb well dried flour, 4 eggs leaving out 2 whites. Rub the sugar and butter together till they become a cream, then add the flour by degrees. Mix all the eggs and flavour with lemon peel. Bake them in small tins in a moderate oven. N.B. a portion of cornflour instead of so much flour makes them lighter.

Household recipe book, Norfolk (early 20th century)

Sweet Things

There's night and day, brother, both sweet things: sun, moon and stars, brother, all sweet things; there's likewise a wind on the heath. Life is very sweet, brother; who would wish to die?

George Borrow: Lavengro.

Patriot

Standing as I do, in view of God and Eternity, I realise that patriotism is not enough: I must have no hatred or bitterness towards anyone.

Last words of Nurse Edith Cavell (born at Swardeston, Norfolk, and buried in Norwich Cathedral. Shot as a spy during the 1914-18 War)

Lines on Lynn

Lynn emerges from the meadows, from the fen, and from the sea...as though a wave had subsided and left its towers uncovered.

Mrs Herbert Jones: Sandringham Past and Present

Every man that lands in Lynn feels all through him the antiquity and the call of the town...You can see the past effect of ownership and individuality in Lynn as clearly as you can catch affection or menace in a human voice.

Hilaire Belloc: Hills and the Sea

Here are more gentry, and consequently is more gaiety in this town than in Yarmouth, or even Norwich itself - the place abounding in very good company.

Daniel Defoe: Tour Through the Eastern Counties (1722)

My Lady Wallgraves Receipt to make Juyce off Liqquorish very good for a Cough or Rhewme

Take a qr of a pound of lyquorish scraped sliced and bruised and two ounces of annise seeds bruised. Steep them in a qr pint of rason water and as much foalsfoot (coltsfoot) water 3 days and 3 nights, then strain out with your hands what you can and set it over a soft fire boyling and stirring it continually till it be very thick. Add 2 pounds of white sugar candy or fine loaf sugar beat it and searce (sieve) it till all will go thro a fine cobweb lawn, and the night before you make it up steep half a spoonfull of gum dragon (gum tragacanth) in a little rosemary water, and bruise a grain of musk and as much amber grease with a knifes point upon a paper as fine as you can with a little searced sugar, and put it to the rest of the sugar a night before you make it up, it will smell and tast ye better. In ye morning pick up ye clearest of ye gum out and beat ye sugar and juyce and gum together in a clean scoured mortar till it be like a past and work it up with yr hands and roul it in pelletts laying ym one by one in boxes or lids then they be dryed in a stove or near a fire wich they must allways be kept near, you must sugar the boxes or lids before you lay ym on.

Elizabeth Ravell: 17th century Suffolk/Essex border

Kelvedon

How pleasant are the meads of Kelvedon,
Where in my youthful days I played at will,
And which I now revisit in my age.
How sweetly winds its little humble river -
Known by its sounding name - the
                      Blackwater -
Through the green level meadows it
                      refreshes,
Where lowing heifers indolently graze,
And sheep repose or idly chew the cud.
The river, when I was the miller's son,
To me was a perpetual dear delight;
But not for any beauty it possessed
That my philosophy was conscious of.
How eagerly I used to bathe in it
When sultry summer days made the earth
                      pant;
But that which most of all delighted me
Were the small fish that glanced within its
                      waters.
How many pleasant hours have I expended
Angling for gudgeons in the pebbly stream,
Myself a happy gudgeon all the while,
The patient votary of distant hope.

James Hurnard (1808-   )

Cholera

½ oz powdered rhubarb ½ oz ground ginger ½ oz ground pepper ½ oz magnesia mix with a little water 1 oz salvolatile and ½ pint brandy. A wineglassful to be taken when attacked. Repeat it if necessary.

Julia R. Spurrell, Pudding Norton Hall, Norfolk (1865)

The Thrush

Mix a small quantity of borax with two tablespoonfuls of honey and give it frequently to the child on a feather.

Julia R. Spurrell, Pudding Norton Hall, Norfolk (1865)

Lines on Norwich

A fine old city, truly, view it from whatever side you will.

George Borrow

The steep and winding lane of Elm Hill, where the slum population of Norwich stew and pig together down ancient courts and dirty alleys.

Charles G. Harper: The Norwich Road (1901)

I should judge this city to be another Utopia.

Sir John Harrington (who invented the first water closet) 1612

This ancient cittie, being one of the largest, and certainly, after London, one of the noblest of England.

John Evelyn

Oh, cytie of England, whose glory standeth more in belly banquettes and table triumphs than in the conservacyon of your antiquities and of the worthy labours of your learned men.

Bale's 'Continuation of Leland's Antiquities'

To Starch and Iron Collars

Put 2 full table spoonsful of white starch into a basin, 1 teaspoonful of finely scraped soap and mix up well with cold water into a thick paste. Add 1 tablespoonful of turpentine, 1 teaspoonful powdered borax, 1 pint cold water. Mix it all well up together. Dry the collars before starching, dip them into the starch, rub it well in and wring them dry in a towel. Have clean hot irons ready, straighten them out and iron 3 or 4 times on the wrong side. Turn them over and iron till dry on the right side. Get a polishing iron, make it hot, dip a piece of rag in clean cold water, wring it and pass it over the right side of the collars so as to make the surface damp. Take the polisher, clean it well, press *heavily* upon it and rub it up and down the collars *quickly* until you get a beautiful polish. Pin the buttonholes together to shape them and put them near the fire or in the oven to air off quickly.

Elizabeth Garden, Redisham Hall, Suffolk (1847)

Hooping Cough

Steep garlic in rum and rub the chest and back well with flannel dipt in the infusion.

Julia R. Spurrell, Pudding Norton Hall, Norfolk (1865)

Colchester

The town looks very nobly from the north
When the descending sun gleams richly on
          it.
There proudly stands the ancient Roman
          castle,
Half hidden by a grove of stately trees;
There is St James's ivy-covered tower,
And there St Peter's lifts his lofty brow,
While old St Mary's rears her battered form,
Telling to all her story of the siege,
Her fine stone tower being topped by vulgar
          bricks,
From whence the one-eyed gunner smote the
          foe,
Until himself in turn was smitten down.
James Hurnard (1808-   )

Mrs Dewing's Receipt for Ringworm

2 drams of tincture of capsicums, 4 drams strong ascetic acid. Rub with the finger gently until the patient feels a tingling for three successive days twice a day. Use neither brush or comb if possible. Then rub the place with rose oil every day for a fortnight and bring off the scurf. Wash the head with soft soap when it will be quite cured. This remedy has never known to fail.
Eliza Savory's receipt book, Norfolk (1859)

Maria's Great Mixture for Weakness

8 new laid eggs well beaten, add a glass of cold water to them and three drops of the oil of cinnamon. Put in a bottle of good port or sherry, sweeten with lump sugar.
Eliza Savory's receipt book, Norfolk (1859)

Lancers Figures

1. Lady and opposite gentleman advance, retire, turn in the centre and finish in their places. 1st couple pass between the opposite couple; in returning they lead outside. The 4 ladies set to the gentlemen on their right, the 4 gentlemen on their right, the 4 gentlemen to the ladies on their left, turn the gentlemen you set with to your places.
2. Top couple advance and retire, advance and leave the lady opposite, then set to her and turn in the centre to your place, advance in two lines on each side, the top couple taking the lady and gentleman on the right and left - opposite couple do the same, each turn their partners to their places.
3. The top lady advances to the centre and stops; opposite gentlemen does the same; they curtsey and bow and return to their places, ladies hands across while their partners go round outside. 1st couple move to the couple on their right then to the couple on their left. The four cross with each other and recross, finishing into places - Chaine Anglaise.

The Grande Chaine. Top couple advance and turn with their backs to opposite couple, each couple advance behind the 1st, the ladies in a line on one side, their partners in a line on the other. Cross and recross with partners; the ladies turn off on the right following each other; the gentlemen turn off on the left, each couple meet up the centre. Ladies advance and retire into line on one side; gentlemen in a line on the other, all turn partners into places.
Elizabeth Garden, Redisham Hall, Suffolk (1847)

Calves Foot Jelly

Boil two calves feet in a gallon of water till it comes to a quart. Then strain it, let it stand till cool when skim off all the fat, and take the jelly up, and if there is any thick at the bottom, leave it. Put the jelly into a saucepan with a pint of currant wine, ½ lb of loaf sugar, the juice of four large lemons, beat up 6 whites of eggs and put into the saucepan, stir till it boils which let it do for a few minutes. Have ready a flannel bag, pour it in and let it run through till it is clean, add the lemon peel when put into the bag.

Eliza Savory's receipt book, Norfolk (1859)

Cochineal

1 oz of cochineal, 1 oz pearl ashes, 1 oz alum, 1 oz cream of tartar. Add the cochineal and pearl ash to 1 pint of water, and boil 20 minutes, then add to the alum and lastly the cream of tartar and boil 5 minutes longer. Let it stand for 12 hours then strain through a muslin and bottle it. It is now fit for use.

Elizabeth Garden, Redisham Hall, Suffolk (1847)

The Great Level of the Fenns

Here thrives the lusty Hemp, of Strength
        untam'd,
Whereof vast sails and mightly Cables fram'd
Serve for our Royal Fleets, Flax soft and fine
To the East Countrey's envy; could we joyn
To England's Blessings Holland's industry,
We all the world in wealth should far outvie.

Here grows proud Rape, whose price and plenty
        foyls
The Greenland Trade, and checks the Spanish
        Oyls,
Whose Branch thick, large and tall, the Earth so
        shrouds,
As heaps of Snow the Alps, or pregnant Clouds
The azure Sky, or like that Heavenly Bread
Which in the Wilderness God's bounty shed.

After long Tillage, it doth then abound
With Grass so plentiful, so sweet, so sound,
Scarce any tract but this can pastures shew
So large, so rich. And, if you wisely Sow,
The fine Dutch clover with such Beauty spreads
As if it meant t'affront our English Meads.

The gentle Ozier, plac't in goodly ranks,
At small Expence, upon the comely Banks,
Shoots forth to admiration here, and yields
Revenues certain as the Rents of Fields,
And for a Crown unto this blest Plantation,
Almost in every Ditch, there's Navigation.

To scan all its Perfections would desire
A Volume, and as great a Skill require
As that which Drayn't the Countrey; in one
        word,
It yields whate're our Climate will afford;
And did the Sun with kinder beams reflect,
You might Wine, Sugar, Silk and Spice
        expect.

Anon (circa 1680)

Ringworm

Mix brimstone and pork lard together to the consistency of an ointment and apply it night and morning. Let the head be well washed with brown or soft soap every morning.

Julia R. Spurrell, Pudding Norton Hall, Norfolk (1865)

Upon a Dog named Fudle Turnspit at the Popinjay in Norwich

Fudle, why so? Some Fudle cap sure came
Into the room, and gave him his own name.
How should he catch a fox? He'll turn his
back
Upon tobacco, beer, French wine, or sack.
A bone his jewel is; and he does scorn
With Aesop's cock, to wish a barley corn.
There's not a soberer dog, I know, in
Norwich.
What...would ye have him drunk with
porridge?
A hundred times, and never touches ground;
And in the middle region of the aire,
He draws a circle like a conjuror.
With eagerness he still does forward tend,
Like Sisyphus, whose journey has no end.
He is the soul (if wood has such a thing),
And living posie of a wooden ring.
He is advanced above his fellowes yet,
He does not for it the least envy get.

He does above the Isle of Doggs commence,
And Wheels th' inferiour spit by influence.
This though befalls his more laborious lot,
He is the Dog-star, and his days are hot.
Yet, with this comfort there's no fear of
burning,
'Cause all this while th' industrious wretch is
turning.
Then no more Fudle say, give him no more
spurns,
But wreck your tine on one that never turns,
And call him, if a proper name he lack,
A four-foot hustler, or a living Jack.

Anon.

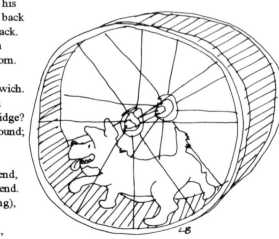

Mrs Durrell's Vinegar

A quart of Gooseberries to a gallon of water, one pound of sugar. Bruise the Gooseberries & put to the water let them stand one day & two nights then strain them through a Cheese Cloth. When done melt the Sugar and turn it up. Green Gooseberries are best.

Elizabeth Hicks (late 18th century) Suffolk/Essex border

Mrs Sacker's Portugal Cakes

Two pounds of Flour, one pound of Currants, one pound & qr of sugar, one pound of fresh Butter, 4 Eggs well beaten, half the Whites, 5 spoonfuls of Rosewater. The sugar and butter must be worked together one hour, then put the Eggs and Rose Water, work it half an hour more, then Flour, Currants and make it into a paste as fast as you can. They must be baked in tin plates having read a Qr of a pound of sugar with Rosewater to ice them in, it be a quick oven.

Elizabeth Hicks (late 18th century) Suffolk/Essex border

For Consumtion

One gallon of milk of coltsfut, burrodge flowers, scabus, sannicel, bonagot, hysop, tunhuf of each one handfull, lickurus, raysons, figs of each 2 ounces, the blood of a sucken pig, 2 pints of snails beaton to pieces with the shels. Stil all those with a could still upon wite sugercande. Drink a quarter of a pint of this 3 times a day.

Elizabeth Ravell: 17th century Suffolk/Essex border

This Will Cuer Loosness

Take a sheeps head with ye wol one it, take out ye brains, bruse ye bonse and boile these in water. Strain it and take half a pint 3 quarters of a pint for a glester.

Elizabeth Ravell: 17th century Suffolk/Essex border

Miss Reynold's Transparent Hair Cream

½ oz of Spermacetti, 2 oz Castor Oil, 1½ oz of Almond Oil, 10 drops each of cloves. Put them into a warm place till dissolved, then with scent and stir till cold.

Eliza Savory's receipt book, Norfolk (1859)

Hair Wash

1 oz borax, ½ oz camphor dissolved in 1 pint of boiling water. Use when cold.

Julia R. Spurrell, Pudding Norton Hall, Norfolk (1865)

To Soften Hands

1 tablespoon of glycerine to ¼ pt, rose water. Shake it.

Julia R. Spurrell, Pudding Norton Hall, Norfolk (1865)

To take Rust off Steel

Rub the steel well with sweet oil and in 48 hours with unslaked lime (finely powdered) until the spots disappear. Turpentine mixed with sweet oil will remove rust from stoves.

Julia R. Spurrell, Pudding Norton Hall, Norfolk (1865)

To Clean Coat Collars

1 oz volatile salts dissolved in 2 pints boiling water.

Julia R. Spurrell, Pudding Norton Hall, Norfolk (1865)

Pike

Boil the pike and let it get cold. In the same water boil macaroni. Take the pike carefully from the bones - mix the macaroni and fish together with a sauce made of flour, butter and milk, pepper and salt and a little cayenne. Arrange it in a flat dish and set in a quick oven to be creamy underneath, brown on top.

Elizabeth Garden, Redisham Hall, Suffolk (1847)

To Clean Paint

Put some Bath Brick to a fine powder - take soap on your flannel, then dip it in the powder and apply to the paint.

Elizabeth Garden, Redisham Hall, Suffolk (1847)

For Bugs

Dissolve ½ oz corrosive sulthinate in ½ pint spirits of turpentine, then add 1½ pints of water. Add this quart of solution of sulthinate to one bucketful of water. With a mop wash the floor and beadsteads and let it run into the cracks. Great care must be taken in using it as it is poison.

Elizabeth Garden, Redisham Hall, Suffolk (1847)